HOW TO HOST THE PERFECT KIDS PARTY

Sandra Wallis

Published in 2020 by FeedARead.com Publishing

A CIP catalogue record for this title is available from the British Library.

WELCOME TO YOUR STRESS FREE GUIDE

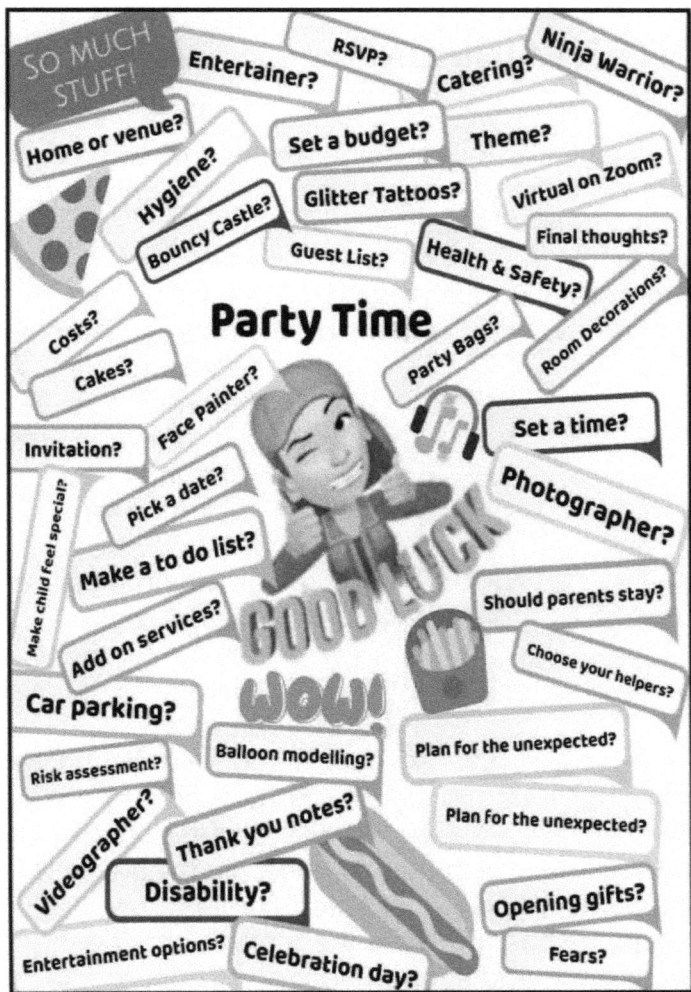

BIOGRAPHY

SANDRA WALLIS
BIG EVENTS
ENTERTAINMENT

I am a Children's Entertainer based in Boston Spa, West Yorkshire. I am married to David and have two children. My business was officially established in 2004 although I started my apprenticeship much sooner. The skills I have acquired over the years have given me substantial hands on experience, in both delivering the right party packages for children and providing a one to one, bespoke service for my customers. I have an extensive commercial back ground and professional qualifications which help to underpin my success in the specialist world of entertainment. My experience has given me the tools to provide the exact advice and support needed to host a successful event and my relationship with the customer has always been based on trust.

4

I am the founder of Free Kids Stuff with Sandra facebook group and creator of Virtual Kids Activities with Sandra on YouTube.

I am also the Author of "The Adventures of Captain Cassie" a unique story with virtual pre-recorded video's to complement the journey!

My business thrives on repeat and word of mouth bookings which fit nicely with my overall aim to reduce advertising costs. This enables me to pass on customer loyalty discounts. My objectives are to deliver high energy events, value for money, professional standard's, customer satisfaction and a safe environment for all.

I currently work in collaboration with several external suppliers and entertainers who provide me with a range of add on services from face painting, balloon modelling, glitter tattoos, marquee hire, bouncy castle hire, soft play hire, cakes, bands, singers, room decor, table wear and helium balloons to beauty treatments. I have recently collaborated with Mini-Epic, electronic party invitations which I currently offer to my customers free of charge when they book a virtual party with me.

I love being creative and innovative putting together new and bespoke party packages, examples of which you will find on my website **www.sandra-entertainment.co.uk**

During COVID-19 entertainers have had to adapt their services to include Virtual Parties. This is something I offer and have gone the extra mile by adding a deluxe virtual party and personalised pre-recorded packages.

I offer a variety of party themes ranging from pirate, princess, alien, dinosaur, family events, DJ, superhero, craft activities, sport, fairy, bubble shows, magic shows to TV and film. I also deliver, bee promotions, puppet shows and school discos My customers include Leeds City Council, Play Den, Italian restaurants, large shopping centres, Asda, BMW, Disney, Bupa to name but a few! I have provided my services to a number of large Yorkshire Festivals over several years working in marquees and on stage as their main Children's Performer.

I operate a small family run business and customer loyalty is the lynch-pin to its success. I have a number of customers who have booked me consecutively over the past 10 plus years which is wonderful because I see their children grow and my customers know they are in safe hands. I am constantly looking for new and innovative ideas. My latest project has been to produce over 30 free children's videos with lots of wonderful activities for them throughout COVID-19. I also produced 2, one hour Summer Holiday videos which have received wonderful feedback.

During August, 2020 I provided a royalty free show for Star Events Online. This enabled them to raise money for 3 prestigious charities and is something I am particularly proud of!

My review's, star ratings, testimonials are exceptional and I have accrued many of them over the years from happy customers. I have also created a few video testimonials for the visually impaired.

I have attended a brief deaf awareness course and I am currently learning some key signs in Makaton (unique language programme that uses symbols, signs and speech to enable people to communicate).

I believe to stay fresh in this industry it is important to constantly change and reinvent yourself. I keep abreast of all the latest children's technology, movies, music and gadgets. My latest acquisition is a huge colourful roulette spinning game which offers the birthday child a multitude of options, ranging from dance routines, party games, prizes, to dares depending on where the pin stops.

I am proud to have been voted one of the top 5 entertainers in Leeds by Families Magazine and I have appeared on TV.

My come back campaign, post COVID-19, will be to offer a bonus for customer loyalty.

CONTENTS   PAGES

CONTENTS   PAGES

9

INTRODUCTION

Welcome to my stress free guide to throwing a successful kid's party! I often get asked "how on earth do you manage to keep 40 boisterous children under control?" or "I couldn't do your job for all the tea in China". To be honest I am delighted that the majority of my customers take that view as it is my job to reduce the stress placed on parents when booking an event. My thirty plus tips will ease you through the process and various steps you need to consider before you begin planning an event. I have occasionally referred to my own website at www.sandra-entertainment.co.uk to further expand on the topics.

Planning a party can be stressful and we all have different tolerance limits but did you know that when it comes to potentially stressful situations, kids' parties actually rank second only to weddings? I cover over 30 key steps aimed at taking the stress out of your event and putting you in the driving seat with all the skills and knowledge you will need to succeed.

So let us get cracking.

What makes me credible and why should you bother to read my book?

This book gives you the power to create the best children's party in a stress free, structured way. I guide you through each of the stages step-by-step and give you the tools you need to become a Ninja Warrior and on top of the entire process.

The tips I have outlined in this book are based on my experience of delivering events over the past 20 years and witnessing some of the pitfalls that could have been easily avoided. My experience as a Specialist Children's Entertainer also gives me the tools to provide you with the exact advice and support you need to host a successful event.

I feel blessed that I love my work so much and that I am able to bring joy to the young children who I have the pleasure to entertain. My reason for writing this guide is to help parents and carers make a special day for their children whilst reducing the stress that they can often feel.

My general motivation when taking on a challenge or organising an activity is that "if a job is worth doing, it's worth doing well".

Understand your goals, stick to them, every day is a second chance and one person can make a difference.

Your child will always remember their first Big Birthday Party – no pressure!

I would like to thank my husband, David for inspiring me to write this book and supporting me throughout the process. Thank You!

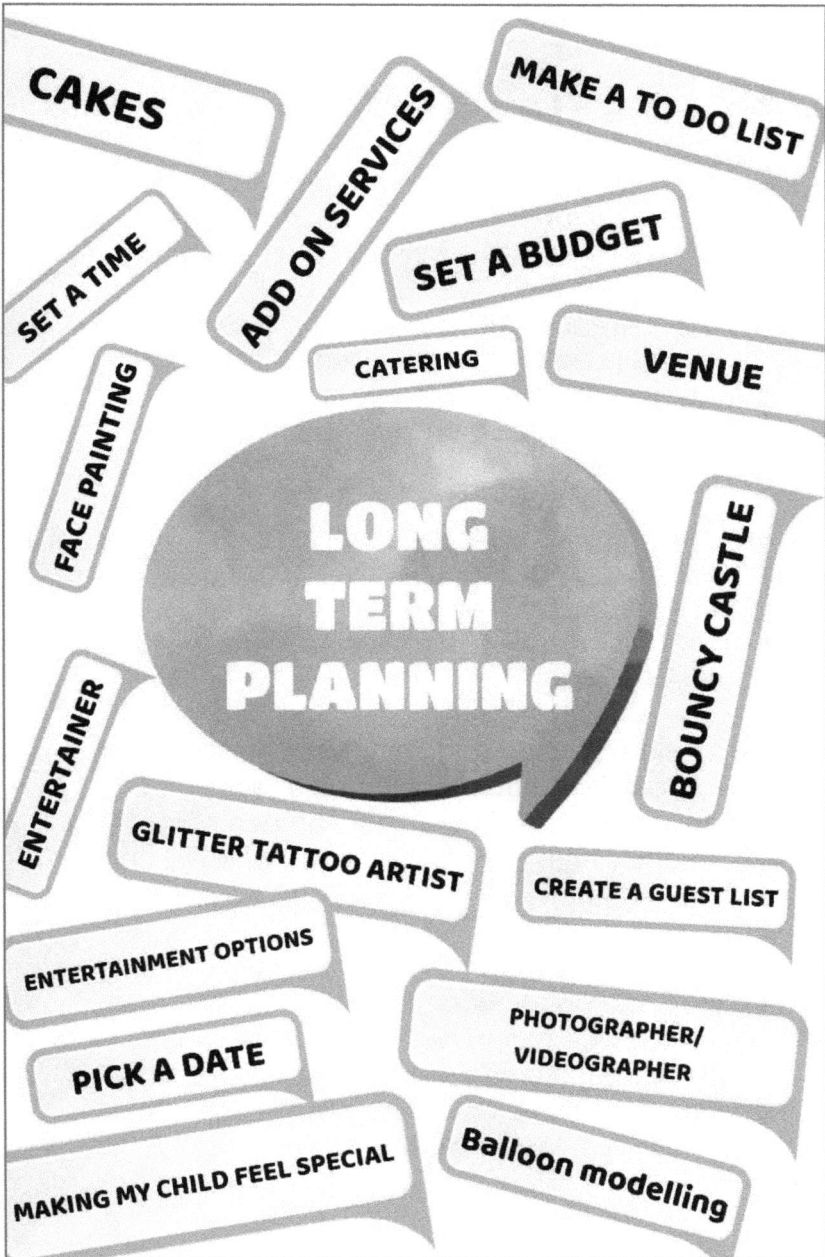

CAKES

MAKE A TO DO LIST

ADD ON SERVICES

SET A TIME

SET A BUDGET

CATERING

VENUE

FACE PAINTING

LONG TERM PLANNING

BOUNCY CASTLE

ENTERTAINER

GLITTER TATTOO ARTIST

CREATE A GUEST LIST

ENTERTAINMENT OPTIONS

PICK A DATE

PHOTOGRAPHER/ VIDEOGRAPHER

MAKING MY CHILD FEEL SPECIAL

Balloon modelling

MAKE A TO DO LIST

Lists are a great way to quickly view the entire actions you need to undertake with lead in times. They support us through the various sections of the event by month, week, day and hours leading up to your event.

They also keep us on track, help us to make adjustments and make us feel in control as we progress towards our event. Lists can be a pick me up as we proudly tick off the sections we have completed.

The flip side, of course, is that they can cause you a little stress if you do not action the tasks on time. It is important to remember that you can allocate roles to other members of the family who will be happy to help out.

It is advisable that you make your lists in a notebook and not on scrap pieces of paper which tend to easily be misplaced. I make lists on my mobile telephone using "notes" and I make sure these are backed up on cloud, just in case my phone is stolen, lost or breaks down.

SET A BUDGET

How much do you want to spend? Costs for kid's birthday parties can add up quickly so it's very important to do a little research before you set yourself a limit. After all if you're not sure what's involved how can you set a realistic budget? Once set, try to stick to it.

My cost analysis checklist will help you reach a decision about your budget and how much you are prepared to spend.

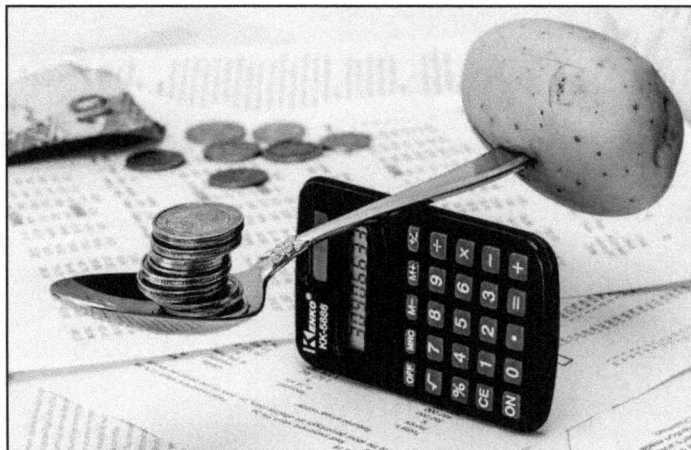

COST ANALYSIS CHECKLIST

1. Cost of venue(s)	£
2. Entertainer quotes	
3. How many children will attend?	
4. Catering	
5. Birthday Cake	
6. Decorations	
7. Party Bags	

PICK A DATE

Be flexible and consider the following;

- Try to book your venue at least 3 months in advance. If not, I would strongly recommend you secure your entertainer first and then search for a suitable venue. Entertainers tend to have a 2 to 3 month lead in time.

- Opt for at least 2 or more potential dates.

- Check availability with at least 2 venues and ask them to hold your dates for 24 hours. This gives you time to check guest/entertainer availability.

- Try to avoid School Holidays and Bank Holidays as this will reduce your guest list.

- Check Brownie, Scout weekends, school trips or other children's activities as this will again reduce the number of children who can attend your party.

- You may also want to book an afternoon slot if the school are hosting a disco the evening before your party to avoid dropout and overtired children.

- Find out who else is having a party that day i.e. a friend in class. This scenario also presents you with an opportunity for a joint party reducing overall costs.

- Make sure key people are available i.e. best friend(s), grandparents and any helpers you may have in mind.

- Accept that not everyone will be able to attend your party.

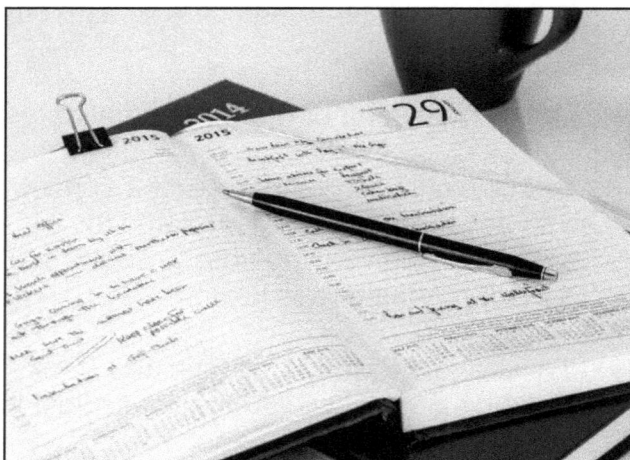

I have provided you with a checklist (Appendix 1) which you may wish to use or adapt accordingly. This approach was something I used when arranging Royal visits to Humberside County Council.

When is your child at their best? Consider nap times – what's best for the birthday child?

Children's parties generally last 2 hours and if you have an entertainer booked you would serve the food sometime within the 2 hour time slot. Allow 15 to 20 minutes for food including the presentation of the Birthday Cake.

If you decide to book your entertainer for one hour you would serve the food at the end of the performance.

Best times for children when providing food at the party

11 am to 12 noon (one hour party)
11 am to 1 pm (two hour party)
    or
4 pm to 5 pm (one hour party)
3 pm to 5 pm (two hour party)

NB: A one hour party can easily be extended to an hour and a half by providing the food at the end of the entertainment.

Not providing Food

If you decide not to provide food for your guests then opt for a slot that doesn't clash with meal times. It's still a good idea to have a quick snack available, just in case i.e. biscuits and juice.

Here are some timings for you to consider when not providing food at your event.

One Hour party	Extended times
10 am to 11 am	10 am to 11.30 am
2 pm to 3 pm	2 pm to 3.30 pm
3 pm to 4 pm	3 pm to 4.30 pm

This is a good option as it clearly reduces costs especially if you are looking for adjustments to make within your fixed budget.

Your entertainer will be able to advise you on the number of hours you should book for your party. I would recommend one to one and a half hours for younger children and 2 to 3 hours for older children depending on the activities chosen.

It is essential that you have an end time, so make it clear on your party invitation and ask your entertainer to play a good bye song. This will indicate to your guests that it is time to leave.

VENUE

When choosing your child's venue decide whether you want to use your own home or book a village hall, play centre, museum, outdoor activity centre, hotel, sports centre etc.

This option will really depend on the number of children you are inviting and whether or not you have to space to accommodate them. If you are hiring an entertainer it is best to speak to them about their requirements and the space you have available. You will also need to undertake a Health and Safety Risk Assessment of your home and may need to add a few more safety measures to ensure your home is child friendly for your party.

Party at home

There are advantages to having your party at home especially if you are a creative person as it gives you days to prepare your home. You do not have to pack food, party bags, cake, drinks, etc to take to another venue and all your equipment is in one place.

This means you cannot forget essentials on the day. It is also cheaper and you have a longer set up and clear up time.

The downside is that it is more work for you. The majority of parents I know thoroughly clean their home before and after the event and they are constantly on watch to make sure their home is not damaged or expensive items broken.

Another problem is that your party can become disjointed and more difficult to manage as children run from room to room sometimes leaving your entertainer without any children to actually entertain. In these circumstances I would suggest you supervise the event and close off areas where children are not allowed to go. It also helps if you make sure the birthday child understands the rules before the party begins.

The majority of parents tend to have their parties at home for children below the age of 3 years and there is so much you can do to help your little one have a fantastic and memorable time.

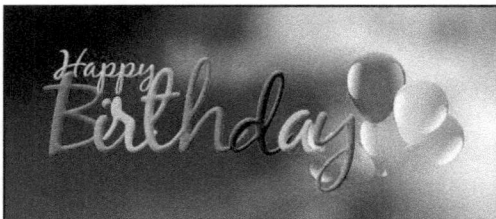

Banners look great at home or at a venue. You can add a photograph, name and date of birth etc.

The photograph below is one example of a wonderful stay at home birthday party with all the trimmings e.g. helium balloons, banners and posters, decorated boxes with the birthday child's name on, cakes with sheep, themed toys to complement the food table and a few simple hide and seek picture games plus a bouncy castle! Children under 3 years love bubbles, nursery rhyme time, pass the parcel and pin the tail on the Donkey. Voila, you have a Party that you can run yourself.

Thanks to Amanda Mayle for the picture above

Virtual party

Another option which is much cheaper than hiring a venue is to book a virtual live event. I'll explain a number of options available to you in the next section.

Hiring a room

If you are thinking about hiring a room it is important to book early because lead in times can sometimes be months in advance or longer depending on the venue you choose.

You will also need to consider car parking facilities, especially if you have someone with a disability attending your event.

Where possible ensure there is a Hearing Loop for any guests with hearing difficulties. I will explain more about disabilities later on.

Once you have booked your room establish their rules e.g. some venues do not like you using blu tack or sellotape on their walls so plan how you will display your banners etc. They may even charge you a small fee for breakages, vandalism, lost items and the removal of helium balloon(s) from their ceilings.   I recall one customer been charged an additional £70 for this service! Admittedly the ceilings were high but this is an additional cost you could certainly do without incurring. Please remember that the removal of helium balloons from the ceiling can be hazardous.

You must ensure all lights and electrical equipment as well as water supplies are properly switched off before handing back the keys to your venue supplier.

If you have a near miss accident or indeed an actual accident at your event you must complete a Health and Safety Accident Report. You can ask your venue supplier for a copy. If a child suffers a bump or blow to their head you should sit them down, comfort them and make sure they rest. You can hold a cold compress to their head i.e. ice cubes wrapped in a tea towel or a bag of cold peas. Some venues have a First Aid box which may contain a cold compress so you should locate this as soon as possible. Seek immediate medical advice if symptoms such as mild dizziness and a headache worsen or perists. You will need to advise the child's parent(s) about the incident and complete the Accident Report Form.

If the child's parents have dropped their child off with you and you feel their symptoms are worsening you should also call them immediately. As previously mentioned, you should provide a guest register for parents to complete on arrival if they are dropping their child off with you.

In my 20 years experience of attending children's parties I only came across the occasional bumps and bruises, nothing too serious so don't get too hung up on these issues. You just need to be aware in the unlikely event of an incident occurring.

Make yourself familiar with the defibrillator, if available, an apparatus used to control heart fibrillation by application of an electric current to the chest wall or heart.

The European emergency number 112 is not the only emergency number in the UK. It is used alongside the national emergency number 999. People with disabilities can contact the emergency services by SMS to 112 or 999 as well as through text relay on text phones or the text relay application.

If the venue supplier is returning at the end of your party to lock up, do not be tempted to leave someone in the building unattended i.e. your entertainer because you are still responsible for both their safety and the venue.

Finally, check all rooms including the toilets are empty before exiting and locking the building.

ENTERTAINMENT OPTIONS

Live Virtual Event?

I've written this book during the COVID-19 pandemic where the Virtual party option became very popular and is a viable option, convenient and cost effective.

Your guests log in using a smart phone, tablet, computer or laptop and password/codes which are provided by your entertainer. This code will prevent someone from accidentally entering your special event. You and your guests/entertainer then appear on the screen and your entertainer guides you through the numerous fun and interactive on screen activities for a set period of time.

The benefits of a virtual party

- Costs less money.
- You can have more guests
- No catering required
- Much less preparation.
- From home
- Worldwide time zones – you can now have friends and family from across the globe at your party!

I would recommend viewing an entertainer's website for any videos of these events and feedback from customers. Virtual events are new to the market which means some entertainers are adapting due to COVID-19. For an example view my website at www.sandraentertainment.co.uk/videos

This is a great opportunity for friends and family to catch up, have fun and interact with an Entertainer taking the lead throughout your event. Virtual entertainment is guaranteed to put a smile on anyone's face with party games, competitions, quiz, action songs, dance routines and more.

If you have a cake you can show this on the camera and let your guests all see the birthday child blow out their candles.

It doesn't have to be a special occasion either, it could just be a "get together" for children who are missing their friends. I have a few parents who have decided to do this and they all split the cost making it a great option for everyone.

Depending on the software used and its capabilities your entertainer may be able to offer you a wonderful keepsake recording of your entire event which your child can watch over and over again. If you would like this video keepsake you **must** ask your entertainer to record it at the start of your party for download later as it cannot be recorded in retrospect.

Virtual Live Stream with a pre recorded section incorporated

This is relatively new to the scene and something I am now offering.   Visit me at www.sandra-entertainment.co.uk/videos to see examples of virtual party options. It may require some searching to find other entertainers who are also offering this specific level of service but it will be worth the effort.

All you need to do is provide your entertainer with some personal footage of your child. This can be a photograph or a video recording which enables you, your guests and your entertainer to view the footage in real time as you watch your pre-recorded section during the live stream. This means you are able to capture your guest's reactions as they respond to the footage.

I also offer my customers a selection of mini pre-recorded videos which are perfect for transporting you and your guests to another scene with quick background changes, as well as an opportunity to introduce another character e.g.Pirate, Princess, Superhero etc. This option also enables your entertainer to interact with your guests during the pre-recording. It is especially useful when point scoring for a dance competition or race against the clock as your entertainer can devote their full attention to how the children perform. Again, you may need to search for an entertainer who is prepared to offer you this Service.

Pre-Recorded video

Again, this is relatively new. You can visit me at www.sandra-entertainment.co.uk /videos

Your entertainer does not appear live i.e. in real time. Your entertainer should provide you with a range of age appropriate and personalised children's activities to be undertaken throughout the recording.

You decide the date, time and place to view your pre-recording. Your entertainer does not appear live i.e.in real time.

Your entertainer is able to make lots of personal references to the birthday child which could incorporate photographs, small video clips of them and references about special toys, events or holiday adventures etc. This puts your child in the centre of the whole party package, making them feel as though they are a super star on their own Television! How super cool is that?

ENTERTAINER

Book your entertainer early to secure the date and time slot you want. A lot of customers book their venue, date and time and then try to get an entertainer at short notice. This is not a good strategy as most good entertainers usually have 2 months or longer lead in times.

To be honest I think most parents could manage a party at home and entertain the children themselves if the children were under 2 years old. I would recommend a few guests e.g. 6 with some soft play mats and age appropriate toys, nursery rhyme time, pass the parcel, a few action songs and some bubbles followed by a picnic.

Do I need an entertainer?

For children of 3 plus years, I would recommend hiring an entertainer as parents often tell me that this takes the pressure off them. The pit falls in doing your own entertainment; especially with high numbers of children is the difficulty in establishing and maintaining control if you do not have the right equipment or skills.

Hiring an entertainer is certainly stress free and they will provide you and your guests with a professional service, control the children in a structured but fun way whilst sticking to your theme and creating wonderful, life long memories which your child will remember for all the right reasons.

Be aware of cancellation fees! Most entertainers should have this information readily available but if you are unsure it is always best to ask.

Below are the standards you should expect from a professional entertainer and the process you may wish to follow if you want to make your event a huge success that will live in your child's memory for years to come and be talked about by your guests for all the right reasons. It is so rewarding for me when I meet teenagers who tell me that the party I delivered for them was their best ever birthday party and that they still remembers it!

Where do I start?

Theme

It is important to understand **your child's wishes** at the time of booking your party. Do not make the mistake of booking something you

would like as this may lead to your child's bitter disappointment on the day with floods of tears.

If you can discuss options with your child then this is the best way forward. Understanding your child's favourite toys, films, character's, activities and their temperament is very important. Remember to be flexible as these can rapidly change by the month, week or even the day.

I offer my customers a no obligation consultation which enables me to deliver a bespoke package that is flexible, can be changed quickly and meets the child's exact needs.

There are so many themes to choose from e.g. pirate, princess, superhero, dinosaur, magic show, puppet show, bubble science etc, etc. Once you have chosen your theme and your entertainer it is time to consider add on services. These may include face painter, ball pool, soft play, balloon modeller, glitter tattoo artist, singer, character appearance, bouncy castle, marquee hire, photographer and party bags. More about these later.

Extracted from my YouTube Channel "Virtual Kids Activities with Sandra"

Cost

Although price is important remember that you pay for what you get. You will be looking for a competitive price structure and once you begin to establish prices you will realise that there won't be too much movement in price between entertainers.

I would be suspicious of any serious undercutting and I think it would be prudent of you to ask why their price structure is out of sync with other entertainers. There may be a totally valid reason for this but it is better to be safe than sorry.

Testimonials

Search reviews, star ratings, customer feedback, any awards your entertainer may have and of course word of mouth referrals.

Testimonials may appear on social media sites and your entertainer's website. I often turn to Netmums for reliable and independent reviews at www.netmums.com

Check the date your entertainer was established

Check how long your entertainer has been trading. Our craft is learned on the job i.e. during an event. The number of years experience is a contributory factor to our professionalism.

It would be fair to say that practice makes perfect and whilst entertainers can do this in front of a mirror it is not the same as having a live audience. The only way to learn from our mistakes is when we are in front of a live audience, "on the job". I was very conscious of this when I first started to entertain and made sure my pricing structure reflected this by offering a reduced rate to reflect my then inexperience. So if your entertainer is undercharging this may be one of the reasons.

Certificates

Your entertainer must have Public Liability Insurance to cover incidents during a performance.

DBS (Disclosure and Barring Service) check is a certificate issued usually to help employers make safe recruitment decisions. There is no longer a legal requirement for entertainers to have this certificate as it is deemed that no child should ever be left with an entertainer unsupervised.

All electrical equipment is PAT, portable appliance tested, to ensure portable appliances meet with legal requirements. Again there is no legal requirement although there are guidelines which recommend that such equipment be checked at least once every 2 years.

Equity

This is an Actors Association membership. Entertainers can apply for membership by providing evidence of their work and skills.

Equity also provide entertainers with their Public Liability Indemnity.

Social Media sites

You can check on social media sites for additional information about your entertainer. Does their website make it easy for you to contact them? Have they uploaded their certificates for you to view? Can you see lots of photographs of actual parties they have delivered or are the photographs taken from other sites and not their own work? Is there any video footage of them performing? All of this will help you to make an evidenced based decision.

Instinct

This for me is the critical component. Do I like them? Are they actively listening to me? Can I get hold of them easily and do they reply within 24 hours? Do they operate a "can do service"? Are they helpful or obstructive? Do they make me feel important? Can I trust them? Can they manage boisterous children and if so how? Do they have good control of the children and is there any evidence of this e.g. reviews or video recordings?

Going the extra mile

- What other services are available to you?

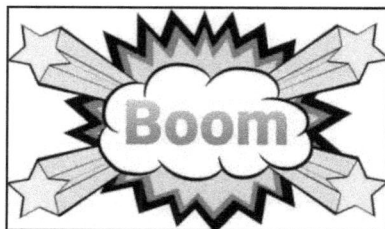

- Are there any freebies e.g.snow machine, printable or electronic party invitations included.

- Will the entertainer add specific games to their package?

- Do they contact you prior to your party to confirm the details i.e. same date, time and venue or has something changed, arrival time, anything specific they should know about your child e.g. very shy, allergies, dislikes, personal preferences for games and theme changes?

- What back up service do they offer i.e. what if your entertainer is ill on the day and cannot attend? I offer an A4 sheet with advice, help and support but in all of my 20+ years I have never had to use it. I also  have a small, reliable crew who would endeavour to step in at short notice should I ever be incapacitated.

- Do they provide bespoke party options?

- Do they bring an electrical back-up system in the event of electrical failure during your event?

- Do they make your child feel special on the day and if so how?

- Do the siblings of the birthday child receive a few extra little treats?

- Do they provide disability and wheelchair inclusive party games?

- Do they use basic sign language e.g. Makaton?

I have included an entertainer checklist for your convenience at Appendix 2.

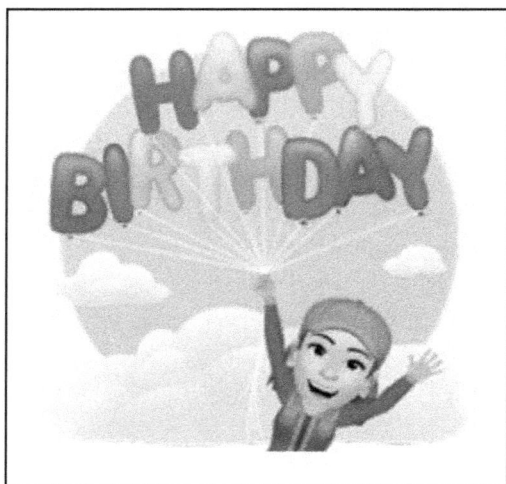

FACE PAINTING

Face Painting is a fun activity that can be enjoyed all year round but it is important to do this safely so that everyone can enjoy it.

Ask your face painter to paint your child first if it is their birthday party and ask for a more intricate design that is not replicated again. Your child is then made to feel special by getting the best design that no one else can have.

How do I find a face painter?

Word of mouth referrals are a great way to secure the right person so ask friends and family if they can recommend someone. You can also search for information on social media sites and websites for photographs of their work. Be careful that the photographs provided are not someone else's work which they have taken from another site.

Ask your entertainer if they can recommend someone as they often network and might even have a small team of suppliers who work in collaboration with them.

I have provided you with a comprehensive face painting checklist for hiring a face painter with additional information about face painting standards at Appendix 3 and Health and Safety Standards at Appendix 4.

Extracted from my YouTube Channel "Virtual kids activities with Sandra". You can subscribe to my channel for lots of creative free kids activities. Just scan the QR code below and don't forget to press your notification bell.

GLITTER TATTOO ARTIST

Hiring a Glitter Tattoo Artist to attend any event puts you on the road to success. They add the wow factor and some artists now offer a selection of wonderful add on services that include stick on unicorn horns, diamonds and lots of bling!

Glitter tattoos are immediately safe to touch without fear of any excess glitter falling off and they are safe to use on children and adults.

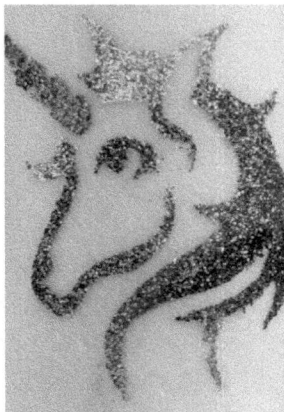

The glue used to apply the tattoos is a gentle, non-toxic, latex-free cosmetic glue made specifically for use on the skin.

To prolong the life of your tattoo, wash it gently with a mild soap, no rubbing with a cloth and pat dry.

Glitter tattoos can be removed by using rubbing alcohol. You can also apply baby oil or lotion on the skin; spread it on the area using your finger and work in a circular motion to remove it. You can use a wet wipe or water-soaked cotton pad to remove the remaining oil and glitter.

Temporary glitter tattoos can last up to 2 months but they look their best for about 7 days from the date they were applied.

Your glitter tattoo artist should only use cosmetic grade glitter that is safe to use on the skin **and NOT cheap craft glitter.**

The *FDA (Food and Drug Administration) requires that decal-type tattoos use only pigments that have been approved for use in cosmetics; this means they are non-toxic and non-allergenic.

Using the wrong glitter can be harmful. A piece of glitter in your eye could scratch your cornea. If left untreated it could become infected and turn into a corneal ulcer, cause discharge, irritation and mild to severe vision loss.

Here are my tips for removing glitter from your eye

- Use your tears. Gently pull your upper eyelid down so it hangs over your lower lashes.

- Flush it. You can also rinse your eye with cool water from a sink.

- Wipe it. If you see the small object on your eyeball, you can try to get it out by gently swiping with a wet washcloth.

- Do not rub your eye

- Seek medical attention if you are unable to remove the glitter.

Your glitter tattoo artist may have a notice advising you about the products used and their contents. If not readily available then you can ask your artist to provide you with this information before your event.

Glitter is something that attracts children. They absolutely love anything which glitters and sparkles. Glitter tattoo kits are very popular and on trend. Most tattoo kits are hypoallergenic and safe for both kids as well as adults which means they will not irritate the skin (even if you have sensitive skin). However, it is always safer to avoid the eye area as the eyes are very delicate and sensitive. There are lots of great colours and designs available for both boys and girls.

Environmental Issues

Some customers do avoid glitter on environmental grounds as modern glitter is usually manufactured from plastic and is rarely recycled leading to calls from scientists for bans on plastic glitter.

*The FDA is responsible for protecting the public health by ensuring the safety, efficacy, and security of human and veterinary drugs, biological products, and medical devices; and by ensuring the safety of our nation's food supply, cosmetics, and products that emit radiation.

BALLOON MODELLING

A balloon modeller, sometimes referred to as a balloon twister, is a wonderful, bright, creative way to fuel children's energy and imagination – they love them!

Balloons modellers use a range of professional balloon sizes, shapes and colours to create a variety of different designs including such things as animals, hats, jetpacks, jewellery, swords, flowers etc.

These are a great add on service at any party and children love them! They are a lovely take home gift and can be uniquely created for each child with balloon colours that can also complement your child's clothing.

It is important to consider the ages of the children at your party. If they are at the younger end I would suggest hiring a balloon modeller who can quickly produce a single balloon model for the children to play with. If you are catering for the older

children then perhaps consider hiring someone who can tell a funny story as they produce a much larger creation e.g. a car large enough to sit inside or an enormous whacky hat for example. This would be a show piece and your balloon modeller could also perhaps teach the children how to make a simple single balloon animal or sword at the end.

Latex Balloons

Fully inflated balloons do not present a hazard to young children, however, burst balloons can be exceedingly dangerous.

Once a balloon has burst, immediately throw away the pieces. Children can be tempted to chew pieces of latex or even stretch them over their mouths to blow bubbles. There is a danger of the latex being drawn into the mouth and subsequently blocking airways.

Your balloon modeller should make parents aware of the risk of choking and display a sign to read as follows. You are very welcome to print this sign and display it at your own event.

CHOKING HAZARD: Children under 8 years can choke or suffocate on un-inflated or broken balloons. Adult supervision required. Keep uninflated balloons from children. Discard broken balloons at once.

If you have hired an entertainer who will be using a microphone you can ask them to make a couple of announcements about balloon safety throughout their performance.

Check that your balloon modeller is using safe material i.e. latex of high quality that is tough enough to resist breakage, easy to use, manufactured and tested with safety in mind. That said, it is important to remember that balloons do burst and some children will become distressed if this happens. Please also be aware that balloons are more vulnerable to the elements if used outside.

Make sure you allocate enough balloon modellers for the number of children attending your event. Ideally, each child should receive a balloon at your party and hopefully there will be a little time remaining for a few extra balloons to be made. This will hopefully prevent any tears, tantrums and complaints due to the inevitability of burst balloons.

If you are providing round balloons to decorate the room or scatter on the floor then never over inflate them. It is advisable to read the instructions for the recommended size otherwise your balloons will begin to self explode after approximately 10 minutes.

Big Events Entertainment

Extracted from my website
www.sandra-entertainment.co.uk

Latex Allergy

Like other natural things people are allergic to
such as bee stings and peanuts, latex can also
cause allergic reactions ranging from minor skin
irritation to anaphylaxis in a very small percentage
of the population.

However, latex allergy does not have to mean
missing out on the joy of balloons as there are
now a number of non-latex balloon alternatives on
the market such as foil balloons and plastic bubble
balloons.

You can let your guests know that there will be balloons at your party by adding it to your party invitation.

Balloon valves

Balloon valves can be inserted into the neck of latex balloons to create a seal without tying a knot. They are a great time and labour saving device, however, they can present a choking hazard because they are so small. You must discard them immediately when balloons burst and do not allow children to play with an uninflated balloon fitted with a valve.

Balloon Sticks

Many balloon sticks come in two pieces; a cup which the balloon attaches to and a stick which attaches to the cup. The cup is fairly small and may present a choking hazard should it become loose. If balloons are to be given to children on sticks it is recommended that your entertainer uses a one-piece moulded balloon stick.

Be aware that children may also use these sticks as swords or to swipe one another. They can be harmful if poked into a child's eye.

Helium

Helium is a natural, non-flammable, non-toxic gas. There is no ecological damage resulting from the use of helium. It can be used safely either inside or outside. Helium is contained in a heavy, pressurised cylinder and always read the safety instructions on your compressed gas cylinder before use.

Inhalation of helium in excessive amounts can cause dizziness, nausea, vomiting, loss of consciousness and death. Helium displaces oxygen in your lungs when you inhale it, which can cause suffocation and you won't even realise it. It can also cause an air embolism (gas bubbles in the blood that can cause seizures).

NEVER inhale directly from the pressurised cylinder as gas can cause the lungs to rupture! Be aware that helium cylinders contain compressed gas, so rough treatment could cause a tank to burst.

As previously mentioned, your venue may charge you an additional fee for helium balloon removal. There are a few health and safety precautions when removing helium balloons so please do consider the following;

- Avoid climbing on furniture or using ladders if you suffer from a health issue, for example, vertigo.

- Make sure someone holds your ladders and only use safe equipment that is appropriate for the task in hand.

- Do not over stretch.

- Do not balance yourself precariously.

- Make sure you have enough people around you to break your fall, just in case you slip.

- If you feel it is too risky do not attempt to get it down. It is better to be safe than sorry.

Can I leave my helium balloons in the car?

It is fine to pick up your helium balloons from the store and take them home in your car but it is definitely not a good idea to leave them in a hot car for a long time. This is because helium molecules get bigger when they heat up, so if your balloons keep getting hotter, they will eventually burst.

*Helium tanks cannot explode. The reason is because the cylinders are equipped with an approved burst disc. In case of any unforeseen circumstances, such as a fire, the cylinder will release gas in a controlled manner and will not explode. Therefore a helium tank can be used and stored at home. Extracted from www.balloongaz.com

BOUNCY CASTLE

There are many suppliers out there and they offer a variety of equipment such as castle with slide, themed equipment, bouncy castle with disco music and lighting and some also offer add on services e.g. marquee hire, soft ball play, soft play equipment, ride on toys, assault courses, sumo suits etc.

Here are a few guidelines to be aware of and the following simple precautions can help you avoid serious accidents at your event.

- If buying or hiring an inflatable for private or public use you should make sure it has either a numbered *PIPA tag or ADiPs (Amusement Device Inspection Procedures Scheme) declaration of compliance (DoC). You go to PIPA or ADiPs websites to check details independently at www.pipa.org.uk and www.adips.co.uk

- It should also have written documentation from a competent inspection body to show it complies with British Standards BS EN 14960.

The photograph above has been extracted from my website supplier at www.funfactorleeds.co.uk

Bouncy Castle Hire and Entertainer booked together

Children absolutely love bouncy castle equipment and will stay and play the hours at a time.

However, if you have hired an entertainer as well they may require you to deflate the bouncy castle during their performance due to generator noise and disruption to their delivery of party games. It might be worth extending your party time i.e. on arrival allow the children to use the bouncy castle for 30 minutes prior to your entertainers performance.

You could also invite family and special friends to stay a little bit longer at the end of the party. This reduces the number of children using the equipment, therefore, making it safer and more fun for the birthday child. It also has the advantage of slowly bringing the event to a steady rather than abrupt close for the birthday child.

This is a good way to maximise your bouncy castle hire and get the best from your entertainer. I have provided you with a few checklists which outline some additional information to be aware when booking a bouncy castle and how to keep you and your guest's safe on the day of your party. I hope you find the following useful.

Safe use of bouncy castle equipment Appendix 5.

Bouncy castle health and safety awareness at Appendix 6.

Fit for purpose on the day - bouncy castle checklist at Appendix 7.

*PIPA is an inspected scheme set up by the inflatable play industry to ensure that inflatable play equipment conforms to recognised safety standards BS EN 14960 which is the only standard for design, manufacture and testing of inflatable play equipment.

ADD ON SERVICES

You may wish to hire a service provider who can supply and match your decorations with your chosen theme. You will need to consider what decorations are required, table wear, catering and

helium balloons. Alternatively, you may wish to purchase them yourself from the internet or a local retailer/wholesaler.

Always read the recommended Health and Safety guidelines to ensure you are operating a safe environment for your guests.

Piñata

A piñata is a decorated figure i.e. animal, flower, super hero etc. containing toys and sweets that is suspended from a height and broken open, using a wooden stick, by a blindfolded child as part of a celebration.

Children absolutely love bashing the piñata and get very excited when it finally breaks away and the prizes fall to the ground. The children rush in screaming and shouting as they pick up as many sweets and toys as they can possibly carry. It is a wonderful add on and really brings the excitement to your party, however, there are a few safety warnings.

I have seen many near miss accidents at events where parents have decided to bring the piñata out at the end of an entertainer's session. There are ways to minimise the risks and I have made some suggestions below.

If using the type of piñata which requires a mask and stick I would strongly advise you to follow the safety instructions on the packaging and in addition to these, here are my tips for safety below.

- 4 or more volunteers to supervise the piñata.

- Create a clear line using chalk, chairs, cones, tape or rope to create a barrier

- Ask your entertainer to help control the children using their microphone.

- Hang your piñata from the ceiling if possible and always stay clear of it.

- Use a washing line pole to hang your piñata and have an assistant to clearly inform the child when to STOP hitting the piñata.

- Another suggestion for holding the piñata safely is to obtain a long pole/piece of wood with a hook in the middle to secure your piñata. Have one person at each end holding the pole/wood.

- Allow one hit per child with the exception of the birthday boy or girl who can be offered two or three hits.

- The piñata I am most comfortable with is the one where the children each pull on a string. A parent will hold back the string which releases the items. They then offer the string to the birthday child who is unaware that it will release all the sweets and toys. This is a very exciting moment for all the children, especially the birthday child as they are the one who released the prizes! This creates much joy and excitement as the children scramble to grab as many items as they can!

Party bags

Children love party bags, full of sweets and toys and they do not really care what is in them, they just want to receive a gift as they leave your party.

Try not to get too worried about the contents of the bag. Here are a few options for you to consider but it is worth remembering your fixed budget as these small items can quickly add up, especially if your guests exceed 30!

- Small plastic toy
- Chalk or crayons
- Rubber
- Pencil sharpener

- Small bottle of bubbles
- Sweets and/or chocolate bar
- Slice of birthday cake

You may dislike the thought of a party bag and in these circumstances a chocolate bar and a slice of birthday cake or pre-wrapped biscuit may be worth considering. It really depends on your budget

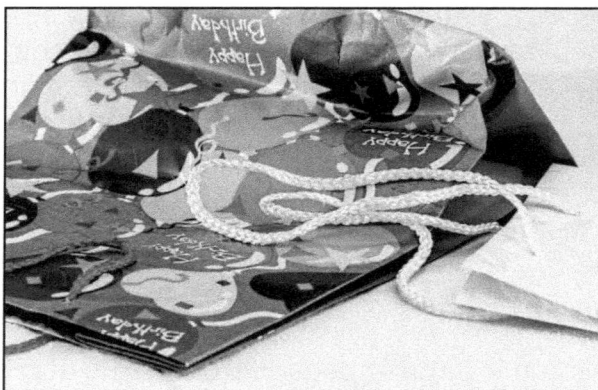

I have known customers hand out Easter eggs, books, puppets, T-shirts, hats, lightsabers, teddy bears and much larger, expensive gifts at the end of their party and some parents, very few, make a decision not to hand anything out.

If you have a craft table it might be worth considering giving the children their finished craft e.g. puppet or jewellery at the end of your party with a piece of cake. This serves as a wonderful take home gift, saves you time and is cost effective.

CATERING

You may decide to use a catering firm or do this yourself. There are a number of issues surrounding food hygiene so here are a few tips which you may find useful.

Food supplied and provided at community events must comply with food standards and be safe to eat. If you handle, prepare, store and serve food at your event on an occasional and small-scale basis it is unlikely you will need to register with your local authority.

It is a good idea to ask parents about any allergies before the party. You can do this on your party invitation or social media sites. You may wish to offer a few alternatives for children with allergies or inform your guests that you would be happy for them to bring their own food if they wish.

How much food should I serve?

In my 20 years experience I would say less is better. I have witnessed far too much wasted food at the end of an event. Children are hyped up and do not eat a lot of food. They simply need to refuel quickly and get back to the party games. A sandwich, packet of crisps and a chocolate bar is sufficient. You may wish to add a few trays of fruit on the table but try to stop yourself going overboard on sugary sweets, ice-cream and jelly. Serving these items slows the momentum of your party and you will lose almost half the children who will not be prepared to sit at the table and wait. It is also putting you under pressure because it is a stressful time getting all those desserts out quickly especially if your helpers have unintentionally abandoned you!

Ask your entertainer when they plan to stop for a break. This gives you time to take the protective wrapping off the food before the children sit down.

Alternative options of food available may include;

- Candy floss hire
- Ice cream van
- Pizza delivery
- Chocolate fountain
- Party pops
- Cupcakes
- Sweet cart hire
- Popcorn maker
- Burgers
- Hot dogs
- Kiddy Cook demonstrations and workshops

Design22._ on Instagram and also listed on my website under catering supplier

Do I need to cater for the adults?

It is quite often a difficult decision about whether to feed your guests at your child's birthday party or not. I have witnessed guests

tucking into their children's food because they are starving and I have seen food wasted because parents have provided adult food which they don't want.

My top tips are as follows;

- Prevent food wastage by making it clear on your invitation that you will also be providing food for the adults.

- Ask your entertainer to make an announcement that hot/cold food is being served separately for the adults and tell them where to go.

- If you do not wish to supply your adult guests with a meal then you could serve biscuits, cake and a drink instead. These are less perishable, cost effective and get around any awkward situations.

- Alternatively, ask your entertainer to make an announcement for adults to help themselves to the party food and supply additional plates to allow for this.

- I would strongly advocate not providing alcoholic beverages at your child's birthday party if you have hired an entertainer. It can make it more difficult for your entertainer to manage the children when the parents and carers noise levels are raised due to alcohol.

The exception to this might be if you have hired, for example, a face painter, bouncy castle, glitter tattoo artist or balloon modeller who does not operate a microphone and need to be heard to maintain control and keep the party going.

- It is advisable to ask your entertainer when the best time for serving hot drinks might be. Be very careful about hot drinks spilling on a child as they can cause severe burns.

*Some of the above information has been extracted from www.food.gov.uk

CAKES

You may decide to purchase the birthday cakes and/or cupcakes from a professional establishment or bake it yourself. There are so many creative cakes available and cake decorating books offering guidance on baking your own.

You could find someone by word of mouth or searching the internet. Well known branded named stores offer a lovely selection of celebration cakes at competitive rates. Always read the food hygiene label to ensure your products are secured correctly prior to and throughout your event.

Lift off cake top

You may wish to host separate parties/gatherings for your child's birthday to accommodate different social groups i.e. one party for close family and another party for friends. If you would like to sing the Happy Birthday song at these gatherings I would recommend a fake cake top. This is a plate which holds your decorated cake top and can easily be removed and replaced on top of another undecorated cake. This is cost effective and if you are making separate cakes at home will save you time as you are only decorating one spectacular cake top. If you prefer to purchase your cakes then ask your supplier if they can provide you with a lift off cake top.

When should I present the birthday cake?

The interval is a good time to present your child with their birthday cake. This allows you enough time to slice and wrap the cake before your guests depart. Alternatively, you can purchase an undecorated cake to slice and wrap the day before your event. This leaves your decorated cake for display on the day and eliminates any pressure you may feel to slice and wrap it before your guests leave. It also reduces the time you will spend in the kitchen away from your child! The advantage of this is that you can use your decorated cake again or freeze it.

The presentation of the birthday cake is an iconic moment for any child and certainly something which will be remembered for years to come. It is therefore important to allocate someone to take the photographs and another person to video record it. Try to make sure you and your partner/husband are also on this iconic photograph.

It is important that you or your entertainer make an official announcement that the birthday cake is about to make an entrance. Make sure you have allocated someone to switch some of the lights off or dim them as the cake makes its way towards the birthday child.

You will also need to be in the proximity of your child to ensure no one else inadvertently blows your child's candles out. You may need to step in quickly to avert this from happening or rectify the situation by relighting the candles as quickly as possible. Make sure you have matches to light the candles on your cake and be careful of any hazards as you carry the cake to the table. It is always best to have someone accompany you to the table to avoid bumping into a child, falling over a toy or slipping on something. It is also best to ask the children to sit down and stay clear of the candles once they are lit as they are a fire hazard and children do tend to get very close to the candles. If the children are seated at the table when the cake comes out then try make sure they do not touch the cake or get too close to it.

I have noticed many different types of candle over the years especially the firework candles. Once lit these festive candles emit a huge shower of sparks for up to 45 seconds and are perfect for birthday celebrations. It is not advisable to place this type of candle next to a child. I would recommend removing the candle from the cake as soon as it has finished as it may remain hot for a little time afterward.

Making cakes

You can serve home-made cakes at community events and they should be safe to eat providing you follow the following standards. If you make a cake at home;

- Use recipes from reputable sources.

- Always wash your hands before preparing food and wear a hair cap.

- Make sure that surfaces, bowls, utensils, and any other equipment are clean.

- Do not use raw eggs in anything that won't be thoroughly cooked, such as icing or mousse.

- Keep cheesecake and any cakes or desserts containing fresh cream in the fridge.

- Store cakes in a clean, sealable container away from raw food.

Storing cakes

You can keep cakes and baked goods with high sugar content in;

- Airtight containers – this will prevent mould growth through absorption of moisture from the atmosphere.

- The fridge – cakes will last for longer but their quality may be affected.

Any cakes with high moisture additions, such as cream added after baking, should not be left at room temperature. They must be stored chilled (in the fridge) and eaten within the use-by date of the added product.

There are some types of icing, such as ganache and butter cream, that can be kept outside the fridge. It is best to store them somewhere cool and dry. Check the guidelines for storage of the particular icing product you will be using.

Delivering cakes to your venue on the day

- Transport cakes in a clean, sealable container

- Make sure that cheesecake and any cakes or desserts containing fresh cream are left out of the fridge for the shortest time possible, ideally not longer than 4 hours.

- When handling cakes use tongs or a cake slice.

Go to www.food.gov.co.uk for more information.

PHOTOGRAPHER/ VIDEOGRAPHER

There are many professional photographers and videographers available to choose from on the internet but again word of mouth is always a good starting point.

There are so many tasks to be undertaken on the day of the event and the burden of these tasks often mean that at the end of all your hard work there are no photographs or video recordings of your child's special day.

To prevent the disappointment of not having a memory captured on the day you may wish to consider hiring a professional or delegating these tasks to a trusted friend or family member. Make sure they film the blowing out of the candles on the cake - an iconic shot not to be missed!

How to gain approval for photographs/ recordings at your event

I have extracted the following article from NSPCC (National Society for the Prevention of Cruelty to children) Learning website

"There is no law against taking photos at public events, including of other people's children.

However, your photographers policy statement should make it clear that parents or carers should gain permission before sharing photographs of videos of other people's children on social media". Ask your entertainer to make an announcement to your guests about taking photographs of their children. Although it is not a legal requirement, it is a courteous gesture. Some parents/carers may have vulnerable foster children in their care or have other significant reasons why they would prefer not to have their children photographed and shared on social media sites.

What if someone uploads a photograph on to a social media site without my permission?

Simply, without judgement, ask the person who posted it to remove it, blur their face or crop it so your child is not in the picture. You may also wish to ask that the photo is not tagged with names and definitely not location. This will limit exposure.

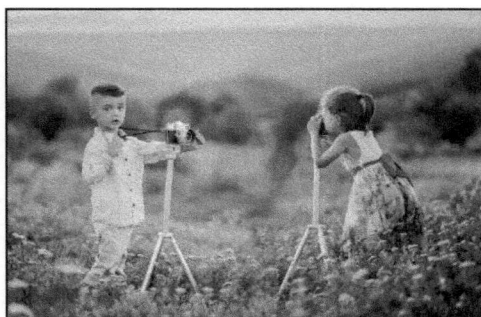

Ask your photographer to provide you with a memory stick containing every photograph taken at your party. It's also worth asking them to create a movie show of your favourite shots.

It is a very important day for the birthday child and you want them to feel special. How will your entertainer do this?

You clearly want all your guests to have lots of fun but you also want your child to feel that it is their special day and and not everyone elses.

Here are a few tips and tricks;

- Ask your entertainer to make some sort of reference to the birthday child at the beginning and then at the end of the party give a big round of applause.

- Ensure the birthday child will always win sweets and prizes *(lots of extra little bits).*

- The birthday child should be the first person to have their face painted and have a bigger, bolder design to include more glitter. The design chosen by the birthday child should preferably not be replicated again

72

- which means your child has the best design on the day. Your child may opt for something smaller and less complicated. That is okay, as long as your child is happy.

- The birthday child will also receive the largest balloon model which again will not be replicated throughout the event.

- They will always be praised throughout the event.

- The birthday child should take the lead in the conga and should always be selected as a special helper, for example, magic tricks.

- The birthday child selects 2 people who they would like to sit next to them at the food table.

- No one is allowed to sit down to eat until the birthday child and their guests have taken their seats – protocol dictates it!

- The birthday child is the only person who is allowed to walk on the top of a play parachute* whilst the parachute is elevated by the crowd. Caution is needed when elevating a child on to a parachute. Make sure they do not fall off the parachute and do not shake the parachute up and down.

- The entertainer can create a wonderful photo opportunity of your child in the centre of a parachute, scene or backdrop**.

- The birthday child should be given first refusal on any games which involve interactive participation with the entertainer.

It is useful to discuss these options with your entertainer and agree a way forward. The more information your entertainer has about your child the easier it will be for them to deliver to your child's needs.

It is important that your entertainer can quickly assess the situation and be flexible enough to meet your birthday child's changing needs e.g. I have had to deal with shy, boisterous, naughty and disabled children who have sometimes needed that extra special support so they get the best from the party. Sometimes children are simply just overawed by being the centre of attention and they need carefully managing.

*Parachute is a colourful fabric canopy which children can sit on, go underneath and use for interactive party games and story telling.

**A backdrop is a painted cloth hung or placed anywhere in a hall or on a stage as part of the scenery. It can have any design and creates the perfect focus for a photo shoot ie proms, Santa's grotto, specific party themes etc.

INVITATION

Your invitation should include date, start and end time, venue with location and an RSVP phone number or email address. You may want to include car parking facilities, disability parking information, catering information e.g. bring your own if allergic to the food supplied. Also include any special requests needed for the party e.g. bring material for robot making or come in fancy dress.

Check with your entertainer to see if they offer party invitations, for example, I offer a free electronic party invitation which includes a photograph of the birthday child worth £4.99. As previously mentioned in my bio I now work in collaboration with Mini-epic .

For electronic invite example go to my home page at www.sandra-entertainment.co.uk

I also offer a paper invitation which my customers can print and send. This has my logo and details already printed on the design which enables customers, parents and carers to contact me prior to the event.

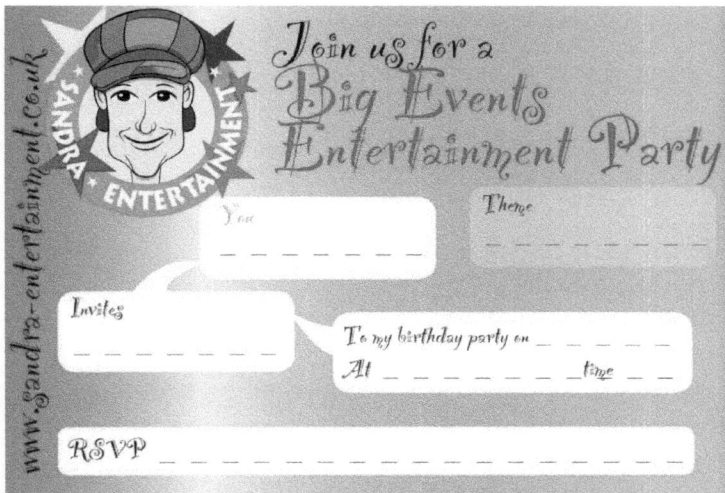

Join us for a
Big Events
Entertainment Party

www.sandra-entertainment.co.uk

SANDRA ENTERTAINMENT

You

Theme

Invites

To my birthday party on _ _ _ _ _
At _ _ _ _ _ _ _ time _ _

RSVP _ _ _ _ _ _ _ _ _ _ _ _ _ _ _ _ _ _

To avoid duplication, inappropriate or too many toys it might be worth considering asking guests to provide gift vouchers for a particular store or book tokens. This might be something you can attach to your party invitation alongside any other special requests.

When should I send my invitations out?

Ideally, you should send your invitations out about a fortnight prior to your party. Too early and parents may forget about it, too late and your guests may already have engagements booked and therefore be unable to attend.

CREATE A GUEST LIST

Younger children

When possible, try to invite the entire class for pre-school children if you can accommodate this. It will avoid hurting someone's feelings and leaving someone out. In fact some pre-schools refuse to hand out party invitations if only a few selected children are invited. If you are unable to invite everyone then you could invite all girls or all boys to reduce the numbers. Some children will cope well with a larger number of children whilst others may prefer a smaller number.

Older children

It becomes more acceptable to invite fewer children as they grow older i.e. close friends, however, be aware you may unwittingly upset someone by not inviting them.

Customers often ask me how many children should they invite? Firstly, you will need to establish whether or not your entertainer charges per head and whether they add a surcharge if the numbers rise above 15 or more. I do not personally make a charge for this but I do warn my customer that the party can become diluted and less personal once the numbers get too high. It is always important to remember that it is the birthday child's event and that is where the focus should be. The ideal number of guests can range from 15 to 30 and once it starts to creep upwards it becomes more difficult to manage, moving the focus from the birthday boy or girl.

What about siblings?

Please be aware that siblings may stay at your party which will automatically inflate your numbers. Don't worry too much about the siblings as they will filter in and out of the party games and your entertainer is only charging you for the actual guests invited.

If you want your entertainer to cater for a mixture of ages then I would suggest you mention this when making your booking otherwise your entertainer will only be providing age appropriate party games for the birthday child which may not suit older/younger children.

At a baby's first birthday there will be a mixture of ages attending and no one expects you to plan any organised party games. However, an add on service for the children is a good idea e.g. face painter, balloon modeller, glitter tattoo artist, soft play, ball pool, sit on toys or a craft table. If you can establish the age range of the children attending it will help you determine which add on service to select.

RSVP

RSVP is an initialism derived from the French phrase "Repondez s'il vous plait", meaning "please respond" to require confirmation of an invitation. This is a significant issue that causes concern, frustration or apprehension time and time again. The majority of my customers ask me for advice about how to get parents/carers to respond. This is a widespread concern and you are not alone. You will have invested a lot of time and energy into planning the perfect party.

It is a worry because you need to know how many children to plan for, for example, sweets, catering, table settings, party bags, the cost of the activity per head, your venue and the entertainer may have asked you to confirm numbers.

Do not forget your child is eager to know who is coming to their party. It can be very frustrating when you have issued your invitations well in advance and guests simply do not respond. It does appear to be extremely rude although some of your guests may have valid reasons for not responding.

How to maximise your response rate

- Send your invitations out about a fortnight in advance and offer a variety of methods that parents/carers can use to RSVP i.e. email, text, landline, and other social media apps. The majority of your responses will arrive by text so do keep track of these (you can use the checklist I supplied earlier to tick who has responded).

- Give a clear RSVP deadline

- Remind parents a few days before your party that you have not heard from them. Do not allow this to cause you undue stress because although the party is the top thing on your mind, it won't be as important to other people. Try not to get too irritated; sometimes people just need a gentle reminder in order for them to respond.

  Parents/carers may have personal difficulties surrounding the date and time of your event. You do not know what's going on in other people's life.

  Your party invitation may still be sitting in a child's school bag or on a shelf at school!

  Most of us do not want to feel that we are harassing people for a response, however, not knowing how many children to expect can be daunting and create problems for you on the day.

- Accept that you won't get a 100% response and allow for some additional children, just in case.

What do I do when my RSVP date has expired?

- Assume they are not going to attend your event.

- Allow for 2 or 3 additional children on the day. You will always have enough food to go around and you could have a few additional party bags available with fewer items in them.

- Try to get some flexibility with your service provider before the event e.g. entertainer, caterer, venue regarding the numbers so that you are not facing additional costs for no shows or anomalies like siblings attending.

SHOULD PARENTS STAY?

Parents begin to feel comfortable dropping their children off around the age of 5. It helps to advise parents whether you would like them to stay or it is alright for them to drop their child off. This is something you can put on your party invitation.

Some children can be overly boisterous at a party and you may already be aware of this. If this is the case then I would suggest parents stay or alternatively you recruit a number of parents to assist in managing the behaviour during the entertainer's performance. This is your child's special day and you have invested love, time and money to make it a huge success. You have recruited your entertainer to entertain, not to be disciplining the same children constantly throughout your event. This is disruptive, stops momentum and reduces the time the children get with the entertainer i.e. less games/less prizes.

A separate room for the parents can be ideal as you need to be aware that parents can also unwittingly hijack the event. They enjoy meeting up with other parents but their constant, loud chatter means that the entertainer you have booked is left with a dilemma because the children struggle to hear and concentrate at the event.

Offering alcohol to the parents can exacerbate the situation.

It is a good idea to create a contact list if parents are leaving their child with you. You will need the child's name, parent responsible and their contact details plus any allergies or medical requirements you should be aware of. Some children suffer from asthma and carry their own EpiPens and know how and when to administer them. However, you may feel overwhelmed if this responsibility is thrust upon you on the day and it is perfectly acceptable for you to ask that particular parent to stay. Alternatively, you could ask your guests if any of them are First Aid Trained. I am First Aid Trained and have to date saved 2 children from choking on whole grapes at parties so it is always a good idea to ask your entertainer if they hold a current First Aid Certificate. It is also advisable to cut your grapes and similar sized food in half to prevent choking hazards.

If you decide that you want parents to stay then I would suggest you put out some chairs alongside the walls for them to sit down.

CHOOSE YOUR HELPERS

Gather your team carefully. Who will be free on the day to help you set up quickly and on time? What obstacles can you foresee? Have you set each of your helpers a task in advance? Giving your helpers tasks on the day of the party will distract you from yours. Tasks to consider may include setting up, clearing up, cleaning up, taking photographs and video recordings, dealing with difficult, poorly, injured or disabled children, accidents, serving food and beverages.

You may also want to consider hiring a helper or perhaps the class teacher/nursery worker to help watch over younger siblings on the day.
It might be a good idea to ask a close family member to help you with some duties when you return home e.g. writing down who bought which toys. This will help you when you write your thank you notes.

Partner

Draw up an agreed list of tasks you wish your partner to undertake on the day to avoid any ambiguity which may lead to upsets, anxiety or frustrations.

RISK ASSESSMENT

A risk assessment is a systematic guide of evaluating the potential risks that may be involved in a projected activity or undertaking.

Proactive entertainers will have a risk assessment especially if they use sports equipment, bouncy castles, ball pools etc.

It's a good idea for you to obtain a copy from your entertainer because some venues do request a copy especially if you've booked your event on council premises/land.

wet
floor

This refers to programmes, guidelines and procedures that protect the safety and welfare of any person engaged in work or employment. The overall goal of health and safety is to create the ultimate safe working environment and to reduce the risk of accidents, injuries and fatalities.
I have highlighted a number of Health and Safety issues already but here are some of my observations from previous events attended and the measures taken to prevent injury.

- Ensure your entertainer has public liability insurance cover.

- Check your entertainers risk assessment.

- Read all health and safety advice provided i.e. from your entertainer, venue or service provider.

THINK SAFETY FIRST

- Adhere to the advice provided by your bouncy castle supplier i.e. make sure you have an adult supervising your equipment at all times and that they have read the guidelines for use.

- Supply of hot drinks on arrival is dangerous and disruptive. Make sure your guests are seated when serving hot drinks or consider offering a cold drink instead.

- Check that all products meet with health and safety standards i.e. provision of face paints/glitters. Cheap glitters contain lead which can get ingrained in a child's eye leading to hospitalisation. Are all products fit for purpose?

- Balloons can cause choking and are especially dangerous for young children who are crawling on the floor unattended. Ask your entertainer to make a couple of announcements throughout their performance to make parents aware of potential choking hazards and ask them to pick up any burst balloons if they see them. In my experience this is something parents are happy to do once they have been informed.

- Catering suppliers must indicate any potential hazards, for example, choking on whole foods. As previously mentioned grapes should be cut in half and certain chocolates supplied around Easter can also cause a choking hazard so do read the instructions.

- Be aware of gluten intolerances, nut allergies etc

- Some religious groups are not allowed to eat certain food/sweets so it is advisable that you supply the correct ones and ask your entertainer to **only** hand these out.

- Smoke machines can cause severe asthma attacks so be aware of potential risks to your guests and make sure your room is properly ventilated.

- Are there correct warning signs provided e.g. slippery floor, tripping over leads.

- Do you have a first aider on site? Do you have a first aid kit?

- If a child has a bump to their head you will need to hand their parent/carer a brief outline about the incident. I have provided you with a notice at Appendix 10 which you can hand out to your guests as and when applicable.

- Do you have an accident report form or accident book? This is necessary for storing evidence of an accident, incident or potential hazard at your event. If you are hosting your event at a venue they will be able to provide you with this.

- Think about safe removal of any helium balloons which may have found their way to the ceiling!

CAR PARKING FACILITIES

When booking a venue it is always a good idea to make sure there is plenty of parking space available for your guests. If not, it is advisable to supply alternative arrangements with a map highlighting key points otherwise your guests may arrive frazzled, frustrated and late.

Protect any disabled parking places if you know that one of your guests will require that space.

Your entertainer will need a car parking area located as near to the entrance as possible. This is because they will be unloading heavy and bulky equipment to your venue and will need easy and quick access.

If you exit a serviceable road which leads you onto a car park, field, stadium etc, for safety switch on your hazard warning lights and reduce your speed to 5 mph until you park your vehicle and switch off your engine. The same procedure should be undertaken when exiting the venue until you reach a serviceable road usually marked on a navigational system e.g. Satnav. This is something you may wish to include alongside your party invitation.

PLAN FOR THE UNEXPECTED

Ask your helpers to stay on at the end, otherwise you may find yourself alone at the venue with all the clearing up to do yourself!

If you have booked a village hall you must remember to read the instruction sheet they provide otherwise you may find yourself charged an additional fee for not complying with their rules.

I would recommend that you collect the keys to your venue the day before. If you are meeting someone at the venue to hand over the keys and go through the specifics e.g. heating system, tea making facilities, lighting etc., I would suggest you confirm everything with them by telephone a few days before your event. Make sure you know where to locate the fuse box in the event of a power surge. Some venues lock their fuse box up in a cupboard so make sure you have access to it. Your entertainer will need electric power for their PA system, microphone, bubble machine and any other electrical appliances.

Give yourself enough time to decorate the hall and set up the catering table. This often takes longer than you think. You will need at least an hour so make sure you allocate and distribute tasks clearly to your helper(s). I would recommend more than one helper as this allows for any unforeseen absence(s) on the day. Some of my customers decorate the room and their tables the night before their party but it is advisable to check that there is nothing else booked in the diary before your event.

You may also want to think about decorating a small table to display the birthday cake on. Quite often my customers place the birthday presents underneath this table. The majority of village halls have enough tables to cater for the number of guests required. However, I have come across the odd venue or two that have a shortage of supplies so I would check with your venue to make sure they can meet your needs on the day.

On arrival you may need to undertake a quick Health and Safety check. The people using it before you may have left some water on the floor or some small hazardous toys which people may trip or choke on. Carpets with rips or curled edges can also be a tripping hazard and best removed wherever possible.

It's often a good idea to take a spare piece of clothing for the birthday child or one of their friends to avoid any embarrassing accidents which may occur.

Not all your guests will RSVP but you are prepared for this so try not to worry on the day. Make sure you have a few spare toys and cake to hand out to unexpected guests and siblings at the end of your party.

Make sure you are able to explain on a map precisely how to reach your venue as some of your guests may find the venue difficult to find. It is important that you check your phone several times leading up to the start of your party so that you can assist the guests who may be struggling to find you.

There will always be tantrums, tears and tiara's and that's OK

Be prepared to ask children or their parents/carers to get their child to relinquish any toys which may be harmful when the party starts e.g. lightsabers, swords, pirate hooks etc. Alternatively, you could ask your entertainer to do this for you. It is better to prevent a child getting injured than having to deal with the consequences afterwards especially if it's the birthday boy or girl who is injured.

I normally make a few announcements over the microphone to the children and find that the majority of them will happily do as instructed. That said, there may be one or two children who will not comply.

If a child is still running around dangerously with their potentially hazardous toy I would suggest that you have a quiet word with the respective parent/carer.

It is a judgement that you will need to make on the day, especially if you think the child could be a danger to themself or others. Do not be afraid to intervene. There is only so much your entertainer can do regarding behaviour and prevention is better than cure.

Some children can be particularly challenging, for different reasons and that is why I have suggested that you select a few helpers to promote good behaviour on the day.

It can sometimes be difficult to manage boisterous children but it is important to remember that you have hired your entertainer to entertain the children not discipline them. A good children's entertainer will use a variety of techniques and skills to keep the party on track.

To recap, to avoid duplication, inappropriate or too many toys it might be worth considering asking guests to provide gift vouchers for a particular store or book tokens.

Having a birthday party and being the centre of attention can sometimes be too much for a child and they may feel overwhelmed. Talk to your child the night before the party about what is going to happen. If you are having your party at home explain that other children may go in their room and play with their toys.

Hide any special toys that your child could not bear to be broken or played with by someone else. Remind your child that there is a reward for good behaviour when the party is over – they can open their presents at home!

If you are hosting your event at a venue it is good practice to stay with your child at the beginning of the party. It can be daunting when an entertainer takes control and your child may feel over-whelmed. If you look relaxed and are happy your child will swiftly follow your lead and ease themself into the party much faster.

DISABILITY

If you have anyone with a disability attending your venue it is a good idea to consult with them prior to your event regarding any special requirements they may have or minor adjustments you could make.

Here are a few things you may wish to consider;

- Are there adequate car parking facilities especially for anyone with a registered disability or perhaps a short term injury.

- Think about any reasonable adjustments e.g. access to the building, toilets, stair lifts etc.

  "Wheelmap" is a fantastic resource for finding accessible venues in your area.

- Have you notified your entertainer of any injuries or disabilities?

- Can all inclusive party games be considered for guests with disabilities and wheelchair users?

- Wheel chair space e.g. does it fit under the table?

- Does your venue have a hearing loop for the hearing impaired? Hearing loops are placed around facilities and broadcast audio to hearing aids through a magnetic, wireless signal, which is received by the telecoil in the hearing aid.

- Has a risk assessment been undertaken for partially sighted guests.

- Can your entertainer use sign language for anyone with hearing difficulties e.g. Makaton? This is a communication aid that uses symbols, signs and speech to enable people to communicate. It supports the development of essential communication skills such as attention and listening, comprehension, memory, recall and organisation of language and expression.

  Click link below to view a few specific and easy to use Makaton words and learn how to sign the Happy Birthday song in Makaton!

  If you like my YouTube Channel don't forget to subscribe and press your notification bell for more resources, information and fabulous free children's activities.

You can view all of these by going to my website at;

www.sandra-entertainment.co.uk/videos or by using the links below.

How to sing and sign the Happy Birthday song in Makaton.

https://studio.youtube.com/video/2O1F_IV-ghs/edit/basic

Makaton with Sandra – Part 1

https://studio.youtube.com/video/JXPQs__7Ycs/edit/basic

Makaton with Sandra – Part 2

https://studio.youtube.com/video/jzQfvloAGy4/edit/basic

Makaton with Sandra – Park 3

https://studio.youtube.com/video/mIPlwTn50yc/edit/basic

- Just a quick recap, the European emergency number 112 is not the only emergency number in the UK. It is used alongside the national emergency number 999. People with disabilities can contact

- the emergency services by SMS to 112 or 999 as well as through text relay on text phones or the text relay application.

- Not all disabilities are visible. You might consider asking your guests when sending out your party invitation if anyone has any special needs you should be aware of e.g. disabilities, injuries, catering needs, sweets etc. Some parents may inform you beforehand but I find most parents let me, as the entertainer know on the day of the party.

The picture above is me at a party signing the Happy Birthday song

CELEBRATION DAY!

HIP, HIP Hooray, it is party day!

Sit back, relax and enjoy all your hard work.
There is no more you can do to change the past
so enjoy the moment.

It is very easy to miss out on your child's birthday
by **not been actively present** because you're
worrying about this and that. You have used your
checklist, planned for the unexpected and you now
have the knowledge to easily adapt and put
something right if it is not on track.

Your child will be running around full of joy and
excitement. Today is a time for celebration, the
day you've been planning for weeks or even
months. You have finally nailed it!

Try to avoid long conversations with too many guests as you may miss engaging in the party games with your child and seeing their smiling face. These are magic moments not to be missed. Parents have said to me that they couldn't believe that the party was over so fast. They were so busy hosting the event that they didn't get a chance to see their little one's enjoyment at the party and watch them play.

Remember it is important that you stay with your child at the beginning of the event.

Give yourself some praise, a pat on the back and a big well done! You have just created a memory in your child's life which they will treasure throughout theirs. You are a Ninja Warrior and I salute you!

Almost there!

FEARS

It is perfectly normal for your child to feel anxious on the day of their party and this may cause them to feel sick, have a tummy upset or headache. Once their party is underway these symptoms normally disappear, however, if they persist, treat them as you would normally.

Some children have very real fears of things e.g. clowns or character appearances ,which other children find fascinating, fun and interesting. It can be distressing for other children, parents and carers who attend your event to see a child frightened, screaming and intimidated throughout the party and it is certainly not the desired outcome you were hoping for.

To avoid this scenario, I recommend you make it clear on the party invitation who will be entertaining your children with their contact details.

As an entertainer I have arrived at a few parties to find a screaming child who does not like balloons or the music too loud. This is something the entertainer can adjust on the day in consultation with the host. I always have an alternative service i.e. I will offer quick stamp ink tattoo's in place of balloon modelling or hand out more prizes or sweets. Your entertainer should be flexible, adaptable and able to make suggestions and be happy to help.

You may also have some concerns or fears on the day but try not to worry. You have done everything you can and it is now time to chill and enjoy the party in the full knowledge that you have planned, prepared and executed everything to the best of your ability.

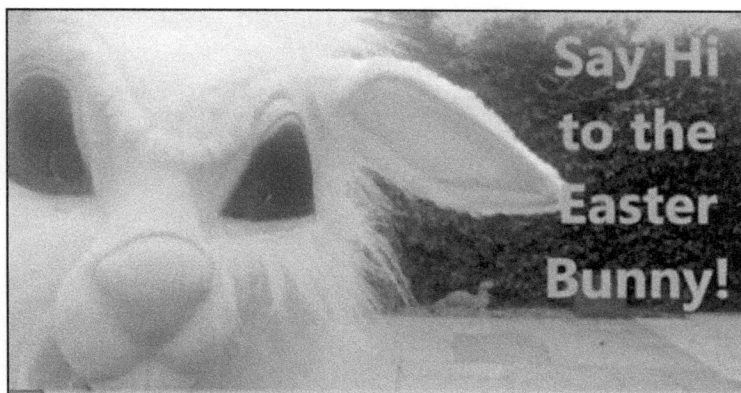
Say Hi to the Easter Bunny!

Opening gifts at the party is disruptive, can lead to arguments and hurt feelings, lost parts and tantrums. Your child will be surrounded by other children wanting to get involved and the emphasis will be on them rather than your entertainer who is trying to engage with them.

Children may begin to tussle for toys and your child may become upset and overwhelmed. It can also make it difficult for you to know who the gift is from which makes your thank you notes difficult to compose.

If someone insists that your child opens their present in front of them, I would suggest you find a quiet room away from other children.

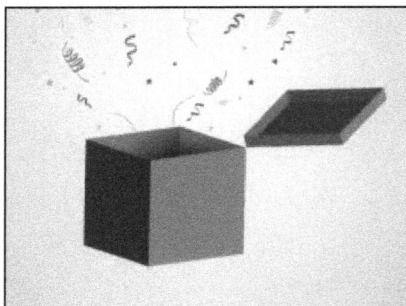

So make sure you write down who gave you gifts. It is also worth thinking about allocating this task to someone else e.g. a close family member or friend.

So, as your pile of presents arrive it is worth allocating an area to store them but do remember to tell your child not to open them until you get home to avoid unnecessary tantrums.

THANK YOU NOTES

Writing a thank you note can often be undervalued. The benefit of writing a note of gratitude is the right thing to do and is greatly appreciated. It is important to remember that the sender also had to go out of their way to purchase and wrap their gift for your child.

Gratitude is good for the brain and hopefully it will make someone's day. It's also an opportunity to reflect and appreciate the time and energy someone has put in to doing something nice on your behalf.

Who should write it?

It really depends on the age of the child but I would recommend that once you finish your message your child draws a scribble or picture on each note adding their own personal contribution. This is a great starting point which will set them up for life. People want to be thanked for their efforts and it's good practice that we teach our children the importance of doing so.

It shows you to be a thoughtful and appreciative person and finally it lets the giver know that you did indeed receive your gift.

NINJA WARRIOR!

YOU HAVE DONE IT!
YOU ARE A NINJA WARRIOR!
WELL DONE!

Congratulations, you're now a party planner and can add another string to your bow!

I do hope you have enjoyed reading my Top 30 plus Tips for Success. You are more than welcome to contact me at;

www.sandra-entertainment.co.uk or by email at sandra.parties@ntlworld.com

My YouTube Channel is called Virtual Kids Activities with Sandra

My Facebook Group is Free Kids Stuff with Sandra

Good luck with your event and have fun!

PICK A DATE
DATE AND TIME CHECKLIST

AVAILABILITY	Venue 1 Date Time Tick	Venue 2 Date Time Tick	Venue 3 Date Time Tick	RSVP CHECK LIST Tick
Entertainer(s)				
Grandparents				
Grandparents				
Grandparents				
Grandparents				
Best friend				
Best friend				
Best friend				
Helium balloon decor				
Room decor supplier				

AVAILABILITY	Venue 1 Date Time Tick	Venue 2 Date Time Tick	Venue 3 Date Time Tick	RSVP CHECK LIST Tick
Caterer(s)				
Marquee hire				
Bouncy equipment supplier(s)				
Ball pool supplier(s)				
Soft play hire				
Face painter				
Balloon modeller				
Glitter tattoo artist				
Other service provider(s)				

REMAINING GUESTS

GUEST LIST AVAILABILITY	Venue 1 Date Time Tick	Venue 2 Date Time Tick	Venue 3 Date Time Tick	RSVP CHECK LIST Tick

ENTERTAINER CHECKLIST

Helpful hints		Response
1.	Name of entertainer	
2.	Theme?	
3.	Fee?	
4.	Reviews?	
5.	Equity member?	
6.	DBS checked?	

7.	PAT Tested?	
8.	Public liability insurance?	
9.	Awards?	
10.	How long have they been established?	
11.	Social media site feedback	
12.	Website structure and relevant information	
13.	Going the extra mile	

14.	What do they do to make your chid feel special on the day?	
15.	Catering for disabilities?	
16.	Any other relevant information	

FACE PAINTING STANDARDS

A professional face painter is someone with a few years experience, lots of practice and operates a clean and tidy workstation. Listed below are some guidelines you may wish to follow when booking a face painter.

1.	How many years experience?
2.	Are they a Member of FACE? Yes/No This is a network of highly skilled and professional artists. You can find more information at; www.facepaintingassociation.com
3.	How fast can they paint a fully blended face? Ideally this should take approximately 10 minutes or less.

4.	Do they offer quick face painting designs? Yes/No
5.	What designs are they able to offer you? They should be able to offer you a wide selection and definitely provide you with designs that match your theme if you have one.
6.	Can they guarantee up to 20 children or more will get their faces painted within the 2 hour period? Yes/No
7.	Will they paint a child's hand, arm or leg? Yes/No Some children are not happy to have their face painted but will let an artist create a design on another **suitable** part of their body.

8.	Do they have public liability insurance? Yes/No This is essential and a **must have.**
9.	Have you checked their reviews? Yes/No It is important to look at star ratings, testimonials and feedback.
10.	Do they have a DBS (Disclosure and Barring Service) police check? Yes/No Although not essential it is nice to have. A face painter should never be left alone with a child so there is no legal requirement for a face painter to acquire a check.
11.	Will they provide a Notice for guests which lists all ingredients used in their products? Yes/No This list should highlight the manufacturer's recommendations on each product and the ingredients they have listed. This is particularly useful if a child has any allergies.

12.	Will they provide information about the maximum length of time a product should stay on the face and how to wash it off?
	Yes/No
	All products must be washed off before a child's bed time.
13.	Does your face painter provide a skin test for guests who have never had their face painted?
	Yes/No
	This can be done by one small brush stroke on the back of your child's hand. If there is no reaction after 10 minutes then it would indicate that it is safe to have your child's face painted.
13.	Are you aware of Health and Safety Standards?
	Yes/No
	If you have circled "No" then I would suggest you go to Appendix 4 Face Painting Health and Safety standards.

Face Painting Health and Safety Standards

- Your face painter must only use face painting products that comply with EU (European Union) and FDA (Food and Drug Administration) regulations. They must be fit for purpose.

- Your face painter should change water frequently and not be adding disinfectant or any other hygiene products to face painting water. Professional products contain agents which act against yeast, mould and bacteria.

- It is good practice to use clean water and regularly change it. My personal preference is to use 3 bowls and dip brush 3 times. I have outlined a basic principal which I adopted to ensure my brushes are clean before use each time.

  - Bowl 1 should be black from dirty paints

  - Bowl 2 should be grey from dirty paints

  - Bowl 3 should be clear

- It is not recommended that children under the age of 2 are painted.

- It is recommended that children aged 2 to 3 years have a small design on the cheek, hand or arm only.

- They should keep their hands clean.

- They must not paint over damaged skin e.g. children with cold sores, eczema, cuts, conjunctivitis, rash, flaky skin, acne, runny noses, cold or flu, lice, chicken pox or any other sign of infection.

- They should not paint over dirty skin.

- They should keep face painting kit and work station clean and tidy at all times disposing of dirty wet wipes, cotton buds and sponges into a bag or container away from their workstation.

- They should use safe glitter, not craft glitter (this can cause serious eye irritation and lead to hospitalisation). They should be careful when using products near the eyes. Some face painters are happy to create wonderful designs which avoid the eye area.

- Caution; when using a director's chair as some small children can slip through the back of the chair. Parents should, therefore, hold their child or stand behind the chair to protect them from falling through.

- It is recommended that painters use a clean sponge for each face painted.

SAFE USE OF BOUNCY CASTLE EQUIPMENT

Your bouncy castle supplier will ask you to sign a Health and Safety disclosure form. I would strongly suggest that you are given this form prior to your party. It will allow you time to digest and understand your legal obligations, responsibilities and to put in place any measures required.

Once you have signed this form you are then responsible for the safety of your guests so it is important to obtain this information prior to your event. This will give you time to digest the information.

It is important to be aware of certain precautions and safety measures you can take prior to securing a bouncy castle. Here are a few questions you may wish to consider asking your supplier before making a decision to book them.

1.	How many children are allowed on the equipment? If you have invited 20 guests then you will ideally require a piece of equipment which can accommodate those numbers. Alternatively, you could consider purchasing 2 bouncy castles or having a rota system in place	

	which is supervised throughout the day. The number of users **should not** exceed the limit given in the instructions as this can cause injuries i.e. bumps on the head, nose bleeds , arguments etc.	
2.	Who will supervision on the day? Children love to climb the walls of a bouncy castle. This may cause the walls of the equipment to fold in and collapse which may trap a child and cause suffocation. A child may also fall off the top of the wall of a bouncy castle causing injury to themself or others.	
3.	Ask your bouncy castle supplier to move the generator as far away from the equipment as possible. In some reported incidents children have cracked their heads open on the generator at the back of the equipment because they have climbed the wall and fallen over the other side.	

4.	Ask your bouncy castle supplier to make sure the equipment is not placed directly next to a wall.	
5.	Ask your bouncy castle supplier to provide you with safety mats at the entrance of the bouncy castle to enable your guests to get on and off the equipment safely?	
6.	If using outside it is best to ask your bouncy castle supplier to provide you with a canopy in case of light rain or safety from UV rays.	
7.	Check that your supplier has enough anchor points for the equipment supplied and that they are using the correct anchors - I have outlined a few of the safety regulations for you at Appendix 6.	

BOUNCY CASTLE HEALTH AND SAFETY AWARENESS

1.	When using outside, all the anchor points **must** be used, with metal ground stakes at least 380 mm long and 16 mm wide with rounded top. They should have a metal 'O' or 'D' ring fitted to the end.	
2.	All inflatables must have at least 6 anchor points. The operator user manual will tell you how many there should be but if you are unclear it is best to ask your bouncy castle supplier. It might also be a good idea to jot down their response in the box provided here.	
3.	If ground stakes cannot be used because of the surface then make sure your supplier has used ballast weights, weighing at least 163 kg with suitable fixings to attach the guy ropes. This will secure your equipment to the ground in the event of a storm. I would suggest you make a note here of the weights your supplier uses.	

4.	The correct anchorage is needed to maintain the shape of the devise and prevent over turn. I would suggest you ask your supplier for this information and make a note of it here.	
5.	Check the blower is safe and has been PAT tested. I would suggest that you ask to see a copy of this before you confirm your booking.	
6.	Check the wind speed; your inflatable will have a safe wind speed and it is advisable that you know what this is prior to its delivery. An anemometer can be used to measure the wind speed so I| would recommend you check with your supplier to see if they have this device.	
7.	Check that your supplier has a public liability indemnity/insurance cover.	

FIT FOR PURPOSE ON THE DAY

BOUNCY CASTLE CHECKLIST

Once inflated and before you use it, carry out safety checks, which include the following;

1.	Has the generator been placed as far away from the equipment as possible?	
2.	Location; is your equipment away from walls or anything protruding which may cause harm to your guests ie tabes, glass, tree branch etc	
3.	Does the equipment have the correct number of anchor points?	
4.	If using weights are they adequate to hold the equipment?	
5.	Is your supplier using the correct ground stakes?	
6.	Are all safety mats in place?	
7.	Is there a canopy (if requested or applicable)?	

8.	How windy is it?	
	Do not use an inflatable in winds above 24 mph which is Force 5 on the Beaufort Scale (small trees and leaves begin to sway).	
	Be aware that some inflatables may have a lower maximum wind speed for operation. Always check the manufacturer's manual for safe operation of your inflatable.	
	A digital anemometer can be used to measure the wind speed so it is advisable to ask your supplier to check this if you are uncertain. You can purchase one of these for approximately £12.	
	NB: You must deflate your bouncy castle if wind pressure increases (as mentioned above).	
	Safely deflate your equipment if the weather becomes unsuitable and make sure all children are asked to disembark from the equipment before it is deflated.	
9.	On arrival check there are no holes or rips in your inflatable	

10.	Make sure your supervisors understand their duties on the day and that you have a rota system which allows for breaks. It is worth noting that some suppliers are able to offer you a member of staff to supervise the equipment on the day of your event for a small fee so it might be worth asking if they can do this for you.	
11.	Finally I would suggest you ask your supplier to sign below to confirm that all Health and Safety precautions have been put in place. These include correct anchor points, weights or stakes have been applied correctly, all equipment is safe and fit for purpose and meets all Health and Safety Regulations and that the wind speed has been checked before handing over the equipment to you. Signature: Date: Supplier/company name:	

FOOD HYGIENE

Additional Information

Allergens

If your activity does not need to be registered as a food business, you don't have to provide information for consumers about allergens present in the food as ingredients. However, it is recommended that you do so as best practice.

Food hygiene certificates

You do not need a food hygiene certificate to make and sell food for a one off birthday party. However, you are responsible for safe handling of any food you serve at your event.

Keeping food safe

Here are some general tips for when you're making food for guests at your event.

- Prepare food in advance and freeze it, if you can, but ensure the food is properly defrosted before you use it.

- Wash your hands regularly with soap and water, using hand sanitisers if hand washing facilities are not available.

- Always wash fresh fruit and vegetables

- Keep raw and ready-to-eat foods apart

- Do not use food past its use-by-date

- Always read any cooking instructions and make sure food is properly cooked before you serve it.

- Ensure food preparation areas are suitably cleaned and sanitised after use and wash any equipment you are using in hot soapy water.

- Keep food out of the fridge for the shortest time possible.

- Food that needs to be chilled, such as sandwich fillers should be left out of the fridge no longer than 4 hours. If you put the food back in the fridge, do not let it stand around at room temperature when you serve it again.

- Provide advice on how to safely redistribute surplus food and avoid food waste.

Food that may need extra care

Some foods are more likely to cause food poisoning than others. These include;

- Raw milk

- Raw shellfish

- Soft cheeses

- Pate

- Foods containing raw egg

- Cooked sliced meats

If serving any of the above foods then please seek further information from www.food.gov.uk

PARTY DAY CHECKLIST

Helpful Hints	Tick
Village hall keys, alarm code and instruction sheet	
Brief helpers/volunteers Any lists of duties which you intend to allocate on arrival	
Catering - food allergy notice Check fridge, freezer, table tops and storage areas. Check lids are sealed tight before transporting food	
Tea, coffee, sugar, milk, alcoholic beverages and juice	
Tea towels/Tea cloth Washing up liquid Cleaning materials	
Birthday Cake Pop cakes Muffins Cupcakes Desserts	
Candles	

Matches/lighter	
Balloons for the floor and helium balloons/Helium canister Safety choking notice	
Party Bags and additional toys	
Craft table accessories (if applicable)	
Table wear i.e. Plates/boxes Cutlery Cups Jugs Juice	
Room decorations and banners	
Piñata, stick and mask allocate helpers/volunteers – make sure you brief them beforehand. Pack either chalk, rope, cones or tape to mark the safe area. Tell your entertainer about the piñata and when you intend to use it. Ask your Entertainer for their help Pole to hang piñata. Hook to hold piñata in place	
Spare piece of clothing	
Phone	

Camera	
Video recorder	
Spare batteries for appliances	
All charging equipment for phones, laptops, tablets etc	
Parking reserve sign or cones for your entertainer and anyone with special needs.	
Parent/carer registration form on arrival and pen plus spare pen (just in case)	
Locate first aid kit and familiarise yourself with the defibrillator if they have one	
Disability and wheelchair provisions	
First Aid box (if taking your own) Ice or cold compress Allocate qualified First Aider Notice for bumped heads (Appendix 10) Locate accident report book on site	
Remind your entertainer to include any free gifts they have promised you on the day e.g. snow machine, medals, certificates or special sweets etc	

Introduce your child and their siblings to your entertainer and ask them to treat the sibling(s) a little bit too	
Bouncy castle checklist Brief your helpers/volunteers about their roles	
Smoke machine – open windows to ventilate the room Make sure the smoke does not set off the fire alarm system!	
Face Painter – Make sure they have a sign about hygiene and safe removal of products as well as a list of ingredients used in their products	
Ask your entertainer to request that all plastic toys which may be harmful be removed from the dance floor	
Ask your entertainer to make an announcement regarding which sweets they will be handing out on the day. It's always a good idea to say that some sweets may contain nuts	
Remember to speak to your entertainer about your child's temperament Gentle reminder to make sure they make your child feel special – what did you agree?	

Clarify the break time with your entertainer and ask them to nudge you 5 minutes beforehand to help you unwrap food or food preparation	
Map – Be clear when giving directions to your venue. You may need to locate a specific street name on your map to direct your guests to your venue. Perhaps it would be worth delegating this task.	
Payments: Who are you paying on the day? Don't forget to collect your envelopes with your cheque or cash for your entertainers, suppliers, caterers etc Make bank transfer(s) e.g. supplier(s)/ caterer(s), entertainer(s)	
Take a deep breath, welcome your guests and try to remember to watch your child enjoy their big day! Your child may need you at the beginning of the party to help calm them down so make sure you are available. If you look relaxed and are having fun your child will swiftly follow your lead.	

A BUMP TO THE HEAD

Seek Emergency Medical Attention if your child or a child in your care experiences;

Unconsciousness, confusion or disorientation immediately after a head injury or after some time has passed.

Also seek emergency attention if your child exhibits the following signs or symptoms following a head injury.

Persistent or worsening headache
Imbalance or dizziness
Vomiting
Memory loss
Mood changes

Thank You

———————————————————   ———————————

Signature   **Date**

SANDRA
BIG EVENTS ENTERTAINMENT

Would like to Thank You for your purchase!

Milton Keynes UK
Ingram Content Group UK Ltd.
UKHW040629280723
425958UK00001B/41

9 781839 454707